The Search for Weasel

Book Two of
The Weasel Chronicles

by KSGreen

To order additional copies of this book, contact:
Xlibris
844-714-8691
www.Xlibris.com
Orders@Xlibris.com

ISBN: Softcover9781599264943
          Hardcover   9781479718665
          EBook   9781664193390

Library of Congress Control Number: 2005907579

Print information available on the last page

Rev. date: 08/31/2021

★ WELL ★

Well ... that was a nice story .... about the weasel and his adventures and his disappearing act and all ...

★ TIME TO THINK ★

I guess i'll have to take some time to think about it all ...

⋆ BLANK BLANK ⋆

Hmmm ... nothing in the Blank about it ....

Maybe i'll get some sleep and worry about it in the morning ...

⋆ SLUMBERING UPON IT ⋆

But sleep did not come easy this tonight ... i tossed and turned over my subconscious ... in that strange land of mystery between waking and not ... i thought ... no report in the Blank ... but how could that be ...? how was it possible ??

how could a weasel just drop from the sky and out of sight .... never to be seen again ... never ... did that mean never as in never ever ?? ... where did he land ?? ... never ?? ... never ever ?? ... never ever land ?? ... i could see this would require some very very extra careful thought processing ... i decided to slumber upon the matter ...

★ HE WEASEL PLAINS ★

And slumbering i went ... slowly i rose above the mundane humdrum of daily waking life ... i entered what is often known as .... and referred to in quiet respectful voices as ... the Weasel Plains ...

a misnomer, without a doubt .... for it is in all actuality ... something altogether different ... higher ... calmer ... a most tranquilted state whereinst resides an intermingled tapestry of weasel thoughts in the very process of being originally thunk .... the nearest translation in the common speech would resound with multiple meanings the nearest approximation of which would be plateau ...

and onto the plateau were flowing troubled and conflicting images ... visions ... but of what ? ...

★ SNOOZE PLATEAU ★

Was i seeing into the future or inside the passed ? ... these were deep questions ... the answers could only be found by delving further onto the uppermost levels of the snooze plateau ....

and there in that strange wilderness ... where blankets float away and pillows transform into salmon fishy squishies ... where angry pussycats grumble ... where favorite silky ties parachute and get tangled onto places where blankets should rest ... where stars float and fish patterns fly off their bedcovers ... there ... i searched ... never quite awake ... never quite dreaming ... never quite quiet ... always disturbed ... always disturbing ... seeking ... sleeping ... seeking ... in an endless cycle of berth ... and re-berthing into higher classes ...

★ MANY BERTHS ★

Let's see then ... by taking it from the beginning ... we will be able to start from there ... my first berth was in steerage .. and although i wasn't very happy, i was good and behaved properly ... so that by the time the time came around for my first reberth ... i found myself in third class .. but having learned the rules of correct auto-karmatic behaviour, i advanced easily from berth to berth ... tourist class ... economy class ... business class ... executive class ... first class ... premier class ... every berth was better than the last until miraculously one day i was awarded with a berth in true weasel class ... i got a great spot very near Vana, this really hot weaselette ... i sort of had a crush on her ... and was content ...

well okay ... i could have been a bit contenter ... i was near the tube ... but Vana was on the tube ... there every night on the nine o'clock news ... doing the spot about all the tragedies ... she always looked so happy ... i sniffed ... what contradictions the world is made of ...

★ PROBABLY IMPROBABLE ★

Controaddictions ... truly ... for gazing at near Vana brought back to my mind my raison and mission for my pilgrimimage to my present place of berth ... why were we here ? .. we were seeking the answer to the ultimate questions again ... how could a well salmoned bonifed weasel just disappear never to be seen again ? ... my hypothesis was that this was highly

unlikely ... in my thesis i went as far as claiming that it was likely probably improbable ... which was definitely sticking my neck out when you came up to it ...

but it wasn't as if i wasn't used to doing so ... ever since i was valedictator for my graduating class at old Weasel State College .. i had been risking my neck on the wrungs of life's ladder ... without actually having it wrung ... i was fortunate ... still i was always creating controverses in my poems about the meaning of life and one weasel's place amongst it all ... so how could i walk away from this present dilemma ?

★ TRY CYCLING ★

Away to go ... you got it ... on the first guess after the question was asked ...

yes ... i could not turn away from such a perplexified pickle ... for if one weasel could disappear .. we all could .. or might at least ... and that was a paranalyzing possibility in the final analysis ... i was near on petrified by the thought ... aghasted that such a thing could happened in real time ...

but i was convicted that .. even though it may have appeared to have occurred .. that that was not what did happen ... not at all ... but there would be no answer in the Blank ... and no solution would be found near Vana because i knew she just read the news and never held a clue about what any of it was about ... but that was her special appeal and what makes her so cute ... i would have to search elsewhere ... i must try cycling to my answers ...

★ AN ENVELOPING CHORE ★

And what a chore i was enveloping myself with ... perhaps i am an optimist deep down around my shoes for i was convinced that i would be able to lick it ... but before i could do that .. i would have to make something stick ... and until i licked it ... it probably wouldn't ... the dilemma was obvious ... but oh yes ... the chore ... that ... that was to seek the answers .. and in order to cover the distance between me and them i would have to amplify my exertions ... i must be obliged to try cycling .. as had been pre-determined earlier ...

they say all weasels must come to Paris ... and so here i was .... again ... ah Paris ... it never changes ... the Chimps of the Lizays ... they were great ... let's all give em a big hand ... what true swingers they are ... then the Mont Martyrs ... dynamite ! ... what great guys always exploding with myrth ... and poor old Les Invalides ... i always felt a bit sorry for Lester ... he never felt very well ...thank heaven's he has his Moaning Lisa to keep him company ... but let us not forget the famous Louvers ... always in amour ... art they not typical of the city of light ? ... the Musee d'Orsay can you see ? ... just lovely ... Paris in the springtime ... would i ever leave you ..? ... hum hum la la dum dum ... what was this wonderful side rue cafe coming up on my right ... Petrol de Parie ... it said lait ... but i was sure i wasn't ... in fact i had been making extremely good time ... there was a full glass ... so i slowed upon my petals and fluttered to a halt ... it looked a bit like a transparent vessel of milk ...

★ TUNNEL VISION ★

When in Rome do as they say .. i say ... but this was Paris where i was roamin' today ... and i was getting low on energy ... so i helped myself to the offered refreshments and pedaled on ... the glories of the culture du les franchisers lost on me ... for i had entered the shady world of tunnel vision ...

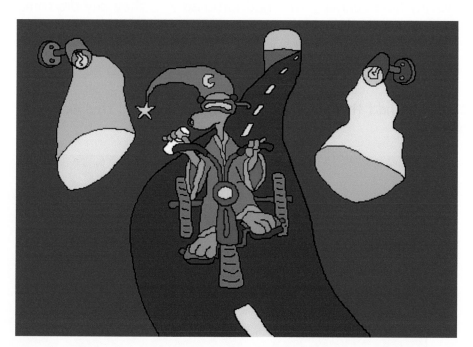

all that was important to me was my mission ... i would seek out new answers to the same old questions ... and boldly go think where no weasel had thunk before ...

★ SPACEY EXIT ★

I came out the other end of the tunnel ... but had no idea where i was ... behind me i felt the shadow of the sun watching over my shoulder ... below i could see such things as Mrs Sippy ... such a grand old gal having a wee mint julep ... Mr Amazoning of the jungles ... working out his way to the seaside ... then yer rope tied up in politiknots as usual ... i was glad

it wasn't my rope ... then there was a freeka nature preserved... a place where people came to partake of the photogeographying of natural resources and wild animal thingys ... above that was the famed cataloony sprained peninsula ... and i could even see my favorite little canary island bobbing in the ocean seas ....

was it a wormy hole tunnel that i had entered ? ... they say anything can happen in Paris ... and it seemed like it just did ... but what a spacey exit , i thought ...

★ MARY'S VIOLET EYES ★

And once again i had thought with rigorous accuracy ... this was a bit of a spacially disoriented pedal ...

as far as i could tell .. i was just passing the moon and venturing about the inner solar system ... let's see ... mary's violet eyes ... Mercury ... Venus ... Earth ... my navigatoring is always impecable ...

★ ALWAYS MADE JOUNIOR STAY UP ★

And right on course ... of course ... here came always made junior stay up ... asteroid belt ... some as large as a school bus and houses ... Mars .. the well red planet ... big Jupiter of the red storm dot and pink moons ... Saturn and the rings of ... and finally Uranus .. the gassy green giant ... no comment necessary here but perhaps a recommendation for some anti-acid tablets for embarrassing après dinner moments ...

i was getting further out here ... i could tell ... for the eternal night was getting darker ... and the sunny sun further and farther away .... perhaps i would just make a quick call at nights and period ... before returning around and swinging home ... the air was a bit thin at this altitude anyway and after all i was still in my night robe ...

★ NIGHTS PERIOD PERIOD ★

The outer reaches of the solar system really aren't very interesting ... nights period ... Neptune ... Pluto ... i mean what can you say ? a long way from home .. not much of a view .. drafty ... icy ... fixer-uppers with not a question about it ... great for weekend getaways but not much more ... the Nep-tune is a bit boring repeating over and over like elevator music ... and Pluto is just like the doggy end of an orbiting sentence ... period .. basically not recommended ... two star at most ... i decided to head home pronto ...

i mailed my tricycle to earth and caught the first express comet going back towards the sun ... much better ... i leave the driving to them and had plenty of time to relax and make up theories ... passing over Jupiter before we gravity swung back into the inner planets ... i made the strangest correalization ... the big red storm dot ... the weasel dot of determination ? ... were these obvious observations just so obvious that no one had never before observed them ? ...

★ MOON LIT COW WEASEL ★

The mail service in our galaxy is light years behind what they have in the Andromedia system ... there i was nearly home with my feet on solid earth ... just braking into moon light gravity ... when what do i see in cocentricyclic orbit but my trusty tricycle ... okay so it went speedy delivery hopping wave crests on the space-time fabric ... but come on now ... the moon has a completely different zip code than earth ... let us acquire some omega bytes of reality here ... snap trap it all ! ... now i would have to get off at the moon and round up my foot powered three wheeler ...

only a few lonely cow weasels would know how i felt then ... watching the comet i should have been on racing towards the bright lights of my home planet ... while i was left out in a near vacuum trying to rope a stray elliptically tumbling cycle ... every 43.8 minutes i would toss out my lasso hoping to snag a handle bar ... why do we do it ?? ... many have asked ... no pay ... no medical benefits ... bad conditions ... the weaselettes love us though ... but its more than that ... there is just something about being under the stars .. standing on a full moon ... its the romance of it all, i suppose ...

★ LUNAR WEASEL FOOT SKIING ★

But this was all distracting from my main thing of the moment ... which was tracking a disappeared weasel from the world famous Weasel Chronicles ... i reeled in my tricycle for i finally snagged it on its umteenth fly by ... i had been counting closely ... seven hundred and sixty-seventeenth ... eight hundred and seventy-eighteenth .. nine hundred and eighty-nineteenth ... ummhundred and humpty dumpteenth ? ... okay .. so i lost count

and rounded it off to the nearest ummth ... is there anyone having a theoretical problem with that ?...

no ? ... good ... may i please continue then ? ... thank you ...

but the most unexpected occurrence occurred ... the more i pulled in on the rope ... the more centripedal acceleration increased ... i started to move forward ... this was great ... let out slow up... let in speed out ... tangential and radial motion were curvilinearating with a satisfactory horizontal displacement resulting in a pleasant first for the moon ... lunar weasel foot skiing ...

★ FLUNG NOT OF PLANS ★

Well ... lunar foot skiing is a cool sport with a lot of sole ... but as those wear down due to the force of friction... things start to get hot ... and they were ... my tootsies were beginning to feel the strain ... they were beginning to glow a bit ... i was searching for some way to slow this whole c e n t r i p e d a l

acceleration thing down ... when to my good fortune up loomed the answer in the form of a natural geological formulation ... a crater ... the sole-ution was pretty obvious ... i would break upon the edge of it ... and stop ... and all would be fine ...

but ... things were not going along the path of plans ... in place of a smooth and graceful slide to an award winning halt ... i lost my footing and was flung ...

★ STAR CAST AWAY ★

And what an inconvenient fling it was ... for i had just begun to weaselize how a world famous weasel like myself could in all sentences of the word have become disappeared ... because ... world famous did not necessairily mean moon famous ... it was all so clear now ... the tunnel vision .. the violet eyes ... mary and junior ... i understood all ... that was why i had came here ... to see that simple funnimental truth ...

but what could i do with my new found moon knowledge now ? ... i was star cast ... as i definitely always thought i should be ... but where was i headed to? ... the tiny dipper ? ... O'ryan's belt ? ... the seven weaselettes ? ... or the great W of Castaweaseopia ? i could only thank my lucky starlets for imaginary constellation lines ... other wise i would have been as lost as my hat ... but wait ... it was on a similar trajectory ... things were looking good ...

★ A MAJOR OOPS ★

Or were they ? ... i had just released myself from the tangled rope that held me and let go of my leash to my tricycle ... i calculated in my weight and robe colour ... the trike's hue and the number of twists in the rope ... pushed a few buttons and read the result ... just as i thought ... it looked like my hat was the center of gravity ... i prepared myself and my vehicle to enter into orbit around the dern thing ... after that i would be able to figure out what to do next ... i was thinking that we could start a new solar system ... and then get discovered by an Argentinean astronomer high in the Andes ... get named .... and then after awhile they would send a mission to see if i was inhabited ... and finding out that i was ... they would bring us safely back to earth amongst great acclaim and pomp ... visitors from another world ... all diplomatic privileges intact ...

vit was a great plan ... but like many of my great plans ... it was doomed to failure ... for i had encountered a major oops ... it was a black hole ... and my nightcap with its two planets was rapidly being sucked into it ... we began to glow with Saint Weaselmo's fire ...

★ PIXILATED ★

A fire i had not seen since rounding the Horn with the well respected Captain Chef at the turn of one of the centuries ... it seemed like lifetimes ago when i clang to the frozen ropes and masts of our doomed ship... a tale of tattered canvas sails and splintery decks ... a salty tale of drifting so'west and crossing the forbidden Antarctic circle ... a tale of and for another time ... but not for now ... now was this tale ... and back to it ... was this the way life had vanished in other major solar systems ? ... one last glimpse of the great M of the upside down constellation Weaseopia and then nothing ? ... it seemed too cruel for comfort ... but comfort was not at the front of my mind ... there were more important things blurring at the moment ...

we were being pixilated as we spoke ... intermingling it seemed with the very lights of existence ... was this really the end ? ... or only the beginning ? ...

many a premise has been speculated about what lies within a black hole ... i had the feeling sensation that we would soon be finding up about it all ...

★ BLACK HOLING IT ★

I expected to be squelched into some kind of unequivocateable inky moosh emanating from the original background radiation of the initial big bang boom ... or something ... seeing how i was being slurppped away into an unfathomable black gravity pit in the heavens ... full of exotic queasy quantummy effects ... and other little nauseating anti-matter thingys ... from which i have heard nothing escapes ... not even after lights out ...

well ... i was feeling like punching someone's lights out ... now that you mention it ... being stretched hither and dither like a rubber band in the far cornerless edges of space was not my idea of a good time ... i was getting pretty annoyed when i noticed a far circle where i was being preceeded into by my hat and vehicular transport ... what was going on ? ... i could see some normalization in my night cap as it slipped through the mysterious barrier ...

★ REPIXILIZED POKER ★

I had been yanked and pulled askew in this strange dark corridor in space ... and was wondering just how could i ever be compensated for such an indignation ?... whom could i sue ? ... when ... i slipped through the barrier myself ... following the rest of my solar system ... and began to rapidly repixilize ... i was in a starlit casino it seemed ... almost convincingly ....

what was this ? ... could this be the center of a black hole ? ... cards ? ... hmm ... i could see my tricycle and night cap had already arrived ... and had faithfullessly made themselves quite comfortable ... the turncoats ... the dealer seemed to be a strange creature with approximately four paws ... two tails ... four ears ... i was beginning to see a pattern ... two noses ...eight or nine whiskers ... one soda ... one sandwhich ... okay maybe there wasn't a pattern ... never mind ... it was of little importance ... for it looked like i was already dealt in ... was it my move ? ... what should i bet ? ... the stakes were high surely ... what was the limit ? .. but Shirley said nothing ... was she bluffing ?? ... i had a royal straight flush in the weasel dot suit ... a very adequate hand ... should i play it close to the chest ? or further from my nose ? ... what if someone had a full yacht in the kitty qat suit ? ... then i would be out of my stash of intergalactic rubles and into troubles ...

★ GO FISH ★

I would bet big .. it made meaningful sensibility ... my old aunty Oop used to say that when i was little ... and it had become an axiom of behaviour for me over the years ... bet big ... but ... i had a moment of extreme doubt ... what if we weren't playing rapid repixilized poker ... what if this was some game i had never heard of ... i decided to play both sides of the deck ...

i tossed out my wager and whispered ominoisily ... go fish ...
and what a knock out bid it was ... old Oop she would be dizzy and proud of me ... the many headed multi-pawed double visioned hydra-tailed creature broke up into two and spun away ... my unfaithful tricycle flipped out ... my night cap folded and dropped out up onto my noggin ... it seemed the potty was mine ...

★ FREE FALL POTTY TRIP ★

But this was nothing new ... i had been going potty since the first day i was bern ... and now it seemed i was totally potted ... but it all comes easy to me for i had been potty trained from an early age to gracefully accept my winnings ... the fabled weasel humbleness ... you see ... well now i had to see what was in the potty ... i hopped upon the table for to sniff out a closer inspection of my booty and ...

it did that old table turns into a pothole trick ... and i fell for it ... well i'll be dang ... i had won a trip ... which i did and tumbled head second into a free fall ... well the trip was gratis so i would expect the drop to be as well ...

★ TRIPPING HOMEWARDS ★

Which it was ... i felt wonderful ... the brand cutting edge new age loosum weight losers dieting program was also included in the compliments ... i felt practically weightless ... they would never believe this at the home boroughs .... it was so easy to shed pounds ... kilos ...grams ... phonograms ... all gone ... but now i could see where the cruise was headed ...

and not only that ... i could see that my tricycle had flipped back into the picture ... it was miracucyclous indeed .... and as fortune would have had it ... we were passing right through the Milky Way too ... well there goes the crash diet ... i thought as i ordered a cone with two

scoops of raspberry and lime iced cream with a cherry a la toppe ... luckily i had won enough spare change to pay for it ...

★ NONCRUNCHABLE POINT ★

And there was plenty of spare time to enjoy it ... i scarfed down the ice cream in normal weasel fashion in zero point zero somethingth of a few seconds ... then washed it down with the cherry ... ah .. now for the best part i thought ... the crunchy cone ... i took a bite ... then another ... but what was this ?? nothing was bitten ...

what was this flipping thing ? ... why did it come with the dessert if it couldn't be crunched up and eaten ? ... i mean ... what was the point of it ?... no matter how munch and hard i chewed ... i could make nary an impression upon it ... was my charm slipping ? ... it couldn't be a hat for i already had one ... then what was it ? ... i nosed in a little closer ...

★ NOSE CONED ★

And as i nosed deeper into the cone thing ... things began to heat up ... the cruise seemed to be heading for a landing near a far south pacific archipelimango ... i could see my tricycle was in trouble again ... if it didn't start behaving ... it would probably

get fired ... luckily for me i had my nose coned ... a light went on ...

oh ... gosh ... what great value these new tours are with everything included and thought out for your every little whimsy and burning desire ... i mean the planning and foresight ... i would write a letter i would ... but now my attention was turning towards a disturbingly likely sudden splashy abruption below ...

19

Paws 1

★ THE WEASEL MERCHANT MARINES ★

Excuse the paws ... but now may be a time to bring up an important subject which has held heavy with my thoughts of recently ... have you found yourself unworkable as of late ? ... and away from it as well ? ... upside down and out but not and about? ... feeling unemployed-ish ?... well there just may be a ray of light in the darkness ... there could be a career opportunity for you !! ... go places ... sea the world ... yes ... all can ... and will unfold right out from under you ... if you just take the oath and sign a few short papers ... and join the Weasel Merchant Marines ... picture yourself within a few short weeks of enlistment ... sharply dressed in your crisp new dress uniform ... formal gloves ... decorated sash ... pin striped cadet slacks ... already entrusted and empowered with the latest advanced technology ...

for example ..take ensign Weasel first class who is seen here field testing the highly classified mobile all terrain LZR laser XO check out counter in your basic text book combat lawn simulation scenario ... not only is he casually comfortable with this multimillion dollar piece of equipment ... but as you can see ... he is also aggressively multi-tasking in a bi-lingual situation by calling for a price check in sub-Saharan Spanish on a pre-packaged net bag of one half dozen Liberian registered yams imported under suspicious circumstances ... when asked ... the ensign humbly stated ... "i had no idea i had this capacity locked up inside me when i was a civiweaselian ... god bless the Unified Nests of Weasonlia and the Weaselonian Free Provinces !" ... sounds demanding ? ... you bet it is ! ... who are we ? ... we are ... The Few ... between ... The Proud ... and ...The Brave ...

Be all that you might have been able to have had the capability of being once upon a time ... now ! ... maybe ... Stand out from your litter when they take out the trash ! ... if you are the one self-starter who is not afraid to grab the trumpet by the horns ... that one weasel in a zillion with the drive ... the courage ... the moxie ... and the courage to drive with Moxie .... the Weasel Merchant Marines wants You !

★ AN ABRUPT ABLUTION ★

An abrupt ablution which would turn into a splat splash at mach 22 .. my approximated speed ... it was something i didn't want to occur in actuality ... or much beyond the serious worry-consideration stage ... but what could a fast falling weasel star like myself do ... i didn't want to become a far away pacific island beach bum burn-out ... i stiffled a sniffle ... this was no good ... a tear trickled from my sunglasses and evaporated in a puff of re-entry heat ... i reached into my pocket and extracted my weasel handkerchief ... it was hopeless ... this time i was really doomed ... but ... but ... then again ... my nose was big enough thank my weaselights ...

yes ... a little damp but it could double as a life saving parahanky ... shoot ! ... why hadn't i thought of it sooner ?... i would have saved myself a lot of drips and snivels ...

★ EYES FOR ME NATURALLY ★

I myself would soon be getting drippy .. but now i wasn't sniveling about it ... for i knew i would live through splashdown ... i was almost safely back on solid earth ... well .. in the sea actually ... but that was close enough considering that a single miscalisthenic of a micro-degree in deep space could have sent me off to visit mary's or violet's or even to their sun's ... none of whom i especially cared to see at the moment ... it was

always eyes for me naturally ... Earth is the place to be ... on land or sea or foam ...

just give me a tall night cap with a star to steer her by ... wind in my sails ... and a water soaked robe ... i ask for so little ... i headed prudently towards the shores of the nearest island ... shorely the right thing to do in the circumstances ...

★ HYPOTHERIORETICALIZED PROCEEDINGS ★

And the circumstances are what we are really concerned with here ... take for instance ... this mister one Weasel of whom our attention has been mingling with throughout his odyssey in time and space ... what if you had been there in Paris, for instance ... say for arguments's sake ... hypotherioretically, that is ... if we were to assume that we were having an argument ... we can make that assumption, for convenience, and to gain a point of reference from which to proceed upon our main premise ... we are at a cafe ... the waitress has brought the bill ... you had a mocha supreme and i had a plain expresso ...quantum leaps of light year spaces that lie in between prices are at stake ... i am on an expense account and you think i should pay for it all ... i say no ... for i don't want to mis-use my privileges ... and you say "oh come now professor Weaselstien ! ... whom cares ?" ... now ... we can all relate to this scenario ... "but," you ask out of naive ignorance, "what does this all have to do with the Weasel anyway ?" ... ah ha ! ... everything ! ... don't you see ? ... its all so simple ! ... had we been standing at Le Petrol de Parie at precisely the right moment ... we would have seen our one mr Weasel simply disappear into the thin nothingness of air ...

but what does the Weasel see ? ... Mary's Violet Eyes ? ... no my friend ... what the Weasel sees is that we and our argument with the bill have evaporated in front of his very nose like something traveling on automagical light pilot ! ...for him to get the telephone number of yonder waitress is no longer in the realm of his real numbers ... so you can appreciate the inherent difficulties of the matter ... or anti-matter depending on one's perspectif ... in any case the Weasel is gone ...

★ PERSPECTIF ★

Well it seems obvious to me, dr Weasenberger ... my perspectif is that if i was the one who had an expense account ... i would surely offer to pay the billette ... the figures added up ... well no account ... what we are really concerned with here is the disappearing weasel hypothesis ... and what might be the matter ...

since the balance must be maintained no matter what ... and no matter what ... matter can not be created nor destroyed ... then ... was a weasel matter ? ... splatter ? ... batter ?... chatter ? ... or what ? ... or could we just conclude that the one afore mentioned mr Weasel never did disappear ? ... and if that were the case then ... we would definitely have to factor in and square

Avocado's number : N a ... hmm ... i guess that stands for not available ... well never mind ... we will use Pi instead ... baked at approximately 314 degrees for just around 3.141592654 hours will give us ... an inconclusive answer ... which means that we must continue the investigation a wee more deeperly ... later ...

★ WEASINGSONG CAROUSO ★

And a wee more deeply is what i was getting into it ... i bumped onto the countless grains of sand that when taken together comprised a lovely wide beach ... but were individually or in small groups quite irritating as they got into noses and ears and other intimate places ... and when wet with salty water stuck all over things like

my robe ... after a day of baking under the hot pacific sun, they were also quite warm unto the toesies and feet ... i hot footed it towards the shade ...

and was rewarded with a wonderfully refreshing coconut ... this was all making sensible reason again ... the evening star was twinkling brightly above the setting sun ... i thought back over my quest ... what a journey i was on ... i was like wee Weasingsong Carouso the lost crooner who was shipwrecked long ago on an island of cancatibuls ...

★ CANCATIBALS ★

Cancatibals ... mon dieu ! ... listen to me ... what was i saying ? ... if i was really like wee Weasingsong Carouso the long lost shipwrecked crooner ... i had better start singing a different tune ... and soon ... i had a crabby audience ... so i chose one of my favorite folk songs ... it was from a cat tonic collection that i knew would tame the savagest of any beasts ...

i quickly tuned my long necked annoyed tortoise shell polynasalesian banjo ... and hit a strum ... i knew this was going to be a difficult show because my instrument had only one string ... my repertoire of course was written in chords ... luckily i did not discourage easily ... i plucked the basic "T" for turtle chord ... which as we all know has only one note ... one of the few musical chords that do ... the jungle was full of anticipation ...

★ GRAND FINE ALLEY ★

And it was not only anticipation that lurked about ... many hungry eyes and ears were following my every move ... i broke into "you are not nothing but anything like an ol' weasel dog" ... a peppy li'l tune i learned early on in my career ... stunning ... i hoped ...

24

and it was ... my audience was spell bound from the moment i opened my vocal chords ... and not long after that they passed out into rapture ... where they remained till the end of my concerto ... i thunged a loud long reverberating "W" chord which i usually reserved for grand fine alleys ... where i was most often called on to perform ... but tonight i played it as an arpegibettergo ... i loosened my turtle-jo's neck and crept quietly off stage ... by the time my fans shuffled off their mortifying entrancement coils ... i would be long gone ... i got music ... i got rid of 'em ... who could ask for any sing more ? ... there would be no autographics tonight ... and to all a good night ...

★ GOOD DUMB IT ALL ★

Good night ? ... but it was way long past the very witching time of night when church guards yawn and heaven's nose who breaths out cajun breath on this world ... aye .. t'was ... and not only that ... but soon dawn would be creepy upon the rosé horizon ... i must manufacture haste ... and quickly ...

i cool footed it down the beach ... in these wee hours the wind was not hardly blowing and the air was not hardly warm ... lucky for me i had a spare one of those feet multiplier special effects to hurry things along .... if i were in .. like .. the book i should be running into my girl Friday at any moment ... good dumb it all ! ... it was Saturday ! ...

why is real life always so boring ? ... when compared with the story ? ...

★ NEARLY UNCOMFORTABLE ★

In the book i could read three or four weeks in less than an hour ... that meant i should already be lounging with my improvised condo minion ... she would be mixing guava tonics and dancing a wee orangotango ... i would be gazing hopelessly out to sea ... dreaming of the world i left behind ... thinking of the problems ... the traffic ... the endless taxes and bills ... the politics ... the tics ... other pests ... by now i would be pouring salted water on my only box of matches so there would be not even the remotest possible opportunity knocking on my conscientiousness about the lighting of a distress fire ... and i would be thinking "why would anyone in their right mind want to be rescued from all of this ?" anyway ...

but instead ! ... here i was huddled around a slow burning coconut fire ... under a palm tree ... nearly uncomfortable ... staring up at a half burned out tricycle ... waiting for dawn to remove the chillies from my ambiance ... these stories just aren't the same in real life ! ... i would have stern words with my editor about this ... this ... this ... did i say tricycle ? ...

★ FIRST AID ★

Yes i did ... i said tricycle ... and there it was ... my tricycle ! ... it was alive ! ... it had survived the re-entry ! ... oh happy days ! ... i was saved ... my minion was three or four weeks away ... and she might not be anything but my imagination anyway ... so ... who can wait around for that long ?? ... i lowered my tricycle from the tree and administered emergency CPR ... cyclic-pyroscoptic-resuscitations ... it coughed and sputtered ... but it would live ... thank heavens !

... but meanwhile dawn was breaking ... and from the catcaphony of noises coming from down the beach ... it sounded like it was breaking all kinds of things ... my audience must be waking up ... i concluded my thoughts thinking that i had better hurry ...

★ A POT FOR SOUP ★

But a few hurried repairs on my trusty tricycle would be of little use ... i could not see myself pedaling around and around in circles around and around this gorgeous lush forsaken beautiful little island with a pack of angry fans on my tail forever ... for one thing what if they just decided to stop ... then i would pedal right into their arms ... and they would put me into a pot for soup ... not very good in the scenario department ... but i envisioned it none-the-more-or-less ...

i had to think about this ... was i born to broth in a stew ?

★ MY GIRL SATURDAY ★

No ... probably not ... born to broth ... it didn't quite have the rebel sound to it that i aspired towards ... but then again ... what a scene for a dramatic last minute rescue ... my girl Saturday would come rushing quietly through the snapping and breaking boughs and twigs of the foliage of the deep dark impermeable jungle ... unsoup me ... and we would find a shallow light permeable spot between the trees and escape ... i decided to risk it ... i liked the sound of it ... it would work ...

and here she came right with the cue ... Saturday ! ... i called ... and although she had a remarkable resemblance to Vana ... she seemed to know to whom i was calling at ...

★ ZAG ZIG FLEEING ★

And so ... away we fled ... zagging and zigging throughout the jungle ... danger always near ... lurking behind any blade of palm tree or frond of grass ... higher and deeper into the heart of darkness ...

within my vivid imagination i could hear the beating of the throbbling volcano ... it seemed to be getting closer and nearer too ... lucky it was only my imagination ...

★ NEAR VANA AGAIN ★

Or was it just my reckless heart ?... beating out its jungle drum of rhythmic wild impassioned weasel amour for being so near Vana ... i had reached near Vana of many a times ... but usually i was meditating in some mysterious higher weasel trance or ... she was in a magazine or ... on the telly or ... up on the silver screen ... i never once imagined that we would be thrown together in such dramatic circumstances in a real life story ... but here we were ... intertwined fates ... intermingled destinies ... racing to the very precipitous edge of the rim of a bubbling south seas island heartland volcano ... with Vana driving her point on ... as was usual for her roles ...

Vana seemed to be urging me forward ... was this some strange witchual what was performed upon weasels ? ... even as the foliage and clouds dropped below us as we climbed higher and more into the fresh noxious strange coloured bubbling fumes of fresh air... the jungle below seemed to be chanting ... me ow ... me ow ... me ow ... witch was strange for the jungle wouldn't be getting the ow if i were to accidentally topple foot over heals into the fiery cauldron ... it would be me ... i would get the ow ... never-the-less i became caught up in the moment ... before i knew what i was considering about ... i could hear my disembalmed thoughts echoing ... me ow ... me ow ... i quickly countered with an impromptu mellow weaselism ... what an opportunity for a roasted mellow marshmallow ... and yes ... i just happened to have one with me still ...

★ NOT GONE WELL ★

Well ... however needless of voice speeching it was to say ... i must have said it anyway ... for i could hear the words upon the air ... this is not gone well ... not at all ... my mellow was now toast ... and i wasn't in the mood for picking a bone with Vana for fright of being clobbered ... what had i done? ... should i say something about falling in lava with her ? ... or would that be too prescrumptious of me ? ... maybe she just wanted to be friends ...

but how could i live with that ... ? i must speak ... for i wasn't magma cum laude for nothing ...

★ MATHEMAGICS ★

And i did ... with much pleading in my voice ... Saturday my girl darling ... what have i done to deserve such sharp treatment ? ... i exaggerated with the theatricals a little because i was trying to avoid the point ... then i chose to speak in the magmatic universal language of true lava ... mathemagics ... when suddenly it came around on top of me in a flash poof ... good great gravy weasel chops ! ... i exclaimed ... that was it ! ...

this was the south type pacific where i was .... which meant ... i referred briskly to my mental calculator ... my protractor ... my compose ... and compensating for possible interference from the marshmellow ... i proclaimed a definite of course !

... sometime last yesterday during reentry i must have passed out ... through and over ... and onto the other side of the international dating line ...

★ FRIDAY AFTER ALL ★

My Saturday gal ... she was my girl Friday after all ... no wondering about why she was annoyled with me ... i was using the wrong dating lines ... do you come here every Tuesday ? ... would actually transpire into ... did i not just see you Monday morning ? ... i know from my readings that no disrespectickled girl such as Vana likes to been seen on a Monday morning ... now this complicated things immensely ... i began by rewinding my envisionings back one episode ...

well ... as far and by large as i could tell ... there was no other way out of this volcanic predictament ... i would have to reverse and delete now ... darn ! ... what rotten luck ... that Vana Friday was really hot ... now i had to let her evaporate ... what a major let up ...

★ KICK START ★

Well ... even let ups have silver linings they say ... but i say they haven't got a rusty clue what they're talking about ! ... although my wonderful wonderings had been deleted away from wonderful Vana ... and i was supposed to be getting the silvery fringe benefit of renewed total focus on the job at hand ... not only was i in a mood now ... but the job at hand was not starting very well ...

even after all the attention i had lavished upon it ... dawn was uponst us as the crescent of the waning moon paled and the stars becamest few and less between ... soon it would be waxing full morning ... and i would be exposed in the flood lights of dawn ... which in itself wouldn't be so bad ... as long as they shown the lights on my right side ... but they hadn't

been getting anything right lately ... we would have to reshoot the entire scene in the studio the way things were going ... over budget and beyond ... i thought to myself ... but what was really the serious matter of concern here was that i was still on the isle of cancatibals ... i executed the executives decision and went for the kick start option ...

★ SCRIBBLED UPON ★

But i knew in my weasel heart that a good kick would not get things running ... i searched around myself ... for so dissatisfactory was the bind that i was in ... that i was afraid my only option would be to fast forward out of it ... but when i looked for the button ... it was not there ... envisionings can only proceed in real time ... there was only an reverse envisioning switch ... and that would do me no good ... because you see ... i had

already wiped my envisionings from the disc to a clean slate ... perhaps if i could enable my purge drive and expunge the background ... i hit a few Ctrl Alt Insert End keys ... gee i hardly ever use those i thought ... then just to make sure ... i punched the Home key ...

hmm ... well things were moving along all right but ... maybe not my style this ... not only had i doffed the background for an unwelcome one ... but the welcome part of the foreground that contained my garment robe had been totally relinquished also ... and ... to add to my indignity in this new setting ... i was scribbled upon ... perhaps if i hadn't hit the Home button ... i hit Return before my tail had a chance to twitch ...

★ SECOND AID ★

I thanked my starry weasel diodes profusely once again ... it had worked ... i was back as quickly as a winky blink ... parallel universes suddenly had obtained a scary parallelizing new meaning for me ... but now i was safe in my robe once again ... still surrounded by cancatibals but i could deal with them easily enough ... with authorative aplomb i held up the weasel finger of no nonsense please ... which always does the trick ... they were dumbfloundered

into inaction and speechlessness ... i knelt to listen to my tricycle ... my diagnosis came quick ...

i must perform second aid ...

it was not serious ... my trikey seemed to be coming around ... and it had apparently found a new friend ... a deserted surf board which was bubbling a little off colour as well ... i could see possibilities here ... envisions even ...

★ THE SURFY BRINE ★

And as i was administering remedy type motions ... and generally looking quite busy with great exemplar countenance ... while holding off a crowd of hostile onlookers with bi-standards ... an envisioning did arrive unto me ... now with that abandoned surf board ... that convenient hammer ... the chisel over there ... some of that cycle polish ... those rubber bands by the tree ... the spare paddle wheel ... plenty of nails ... hmm ... maybe just a splash of fresh paint here and thither ... ahh ... she was looking better than new ... i tacked the vulture head figurehead unto the prow ... i was ready ... by the time the sun came tip toeing behind the silhouetted mountainy island and barfed * its rays across the tips of the chip choppy swells ... i would be safely launched into my latest envision ... and upon the waves of the surfy brine ...

and when that sunshine came spewing ** across the morn ... regurgitating *** its warmth over the sea ... i was way out there ... wherest to now ? ... i knew not ... i thought ... so i thought again ... and i knew naught again ... but though my voyage was still going on in mystery ...i had learned of many things in my quest for the clarification of the hows and ways into which an unsuspecting weasel could simply disappear ...

* in weasel there is no negative conoconcoction of this word
** or of this one with the other one
*** or of this one with either or both of the other ones

★ MERMINION ★

For example ... had my condo minion been there at the proper moment in my last envisionment with my chilled coconut guava tonic concoction ... i myself might have dropped off the face of standard existence ... never to be seen again ... disappeared into paradise would have read my well tanned epidermitaph ... well ... never mind ... perhaps next time ... but for now i would set my sights on top of more noble and lofty matters such as ... as ... mon adieu ! ...

were not my eyes deceiving me ? ... for there in the churning waves ... brightly lit by the retching* sunlight ... was Vana again .. garbbled in the timeless robes of the mythical vixen of the seven seas ... a merminion ... and withinst her hand's clutch wast a chilled coconut guava tonic concoction ... !

* see afore mentioned note

★ KRIKEY AND SCYLLIE CHARYBDIS ★

By Krikey and Scyllie Charybdis ... what a hazardous messina straight navigational narrative was happening here ... everything had been going so well too ... but a merminion of all things !... the sirens were wailing at my ears ... whipped into a frenzy by the mild relentless breeze ... i clutched my ears ... and reverted my eyes to another viewing port ... but it was no good ... all hands upon the deck ! ... i sternly commanded ... and they both showed up pronto ... great things were becoming tangled with insight of the balance ... i knew not at which direction the scales would tipple ... i puckered up my courage and ordered myself to be bound with sturdy rope to the handle bars ... my faithful hands complied ...

and the tempest blew ... my paddle wheel was torn asunder ... i was cast adrift uponst the mercy of the seas ... mercy me ! ... but with hands bound ... i would not succumb to the temptstress ... nor to her song which was bored on the gusts ...

Paws 2

★ UNWWMM ★

Pardon the intrusion ... but much has been argued and said for and about being prepared for any imaginal situation ... and true to our motto .. Semper Buy .. the United Nests of Weaslonia Weasel Merchant Marines are ... always ... take ensign Weasel first class ... seen below in a computersized training simulation ...

he has been fed up with all the pertinent facts for the matter at hand ... illegal bargain hunters have

been observed in lawn ornaments and accessories ... a big no-small-matter type threat since bargains are often poached to near extinction ... he is in constant contact with code name Control via the super-hushed-up digital communications Speaking-To-Each-Other-Radio STEOR system ... note the weasel sock of determination attached to his antenna ... an old boot camp prank used in the real field to lighten the spirits ... it is a worst case scenario ... a deserted handbasket has been located in the middle of an isle ... Control has no option but to send him in ... full florescent tubes blaze down mercilessly ... ensign Weasel clutches the standard issue state-of-the-arts lime green portable hand holdable analogical bar-code scanner with avocado accents ... but this is what he has been trained for ... a quick murmur with Control ... and the controversial lost samurai Japanese fan out ploy is deployed ...

is it hard to imagine yourself in such a position ? well the Weasel Merchant Marines are not for every John Weasel Doe Dick and Harry ... but if you are that one Weaseldoe in a mega-zillion-quadrillion ... the UNWWMM wants YOU !!

★ USELESSEASE ODDITY ★

But i would succumb into yonder mythful whirlpool inst to which i was rapidly approaching a definite state of suction ... if i did not hurry up with a plan of some kind my coconut guava tonic would be the first to go ... even the fishes fled ...

i asked myself what would Uselessease Weasel had done in similar circumstances to save his sorry neck ? ... i quickly re-christened my tricycle the Oddity just in case ... that would help if i could not think of anything better ...

★ ENTWANGLED IN SWIRLS ★

But it did not ... and i could not ... i was just about thunk out ... and so my fate became entwangled in the swirls .... once again i had discovered another way a weasel could disappear and never be in the scene again ... but i was not buying this as the grand finale by any means or ways ... even though once again ... i was in way over my head and below my feet ...

i could see amongst the waters merVana ... and she was coming my way ... as i spun down into the depths i held my breath and rationed my last gulp of oxygen ... i would save my air for better times ... like when i needed it ...

★ WEASLANTIS ★

And i needed it now ! ... only there wasn't much left ... below me i could see the spires of the long lost city of Weaslantis ... so that's where it had gotten to ... from my education i recollected that it had vanished sometime ago in the Great Depression ... i have always believed that the Great Depression was just a mythical bad mood ... but now my beliefs were sinking into question in view of the facts below ...

merVana was beckoning me ... as if saying "come into my waterful condo oh Weasel and we can have a splash of fermented fruit juice ... or something" ... it was the or something that had my suspicions up ... something was fishy about it all ...

★ BUBBLED UP ★

Fishy ... and breathless ... Vana always did that to me ... even when she appeared in the merweasel formula ... but of course she was oblivious to it all ... a merweaselette always has that option ... plus she could breath underwater ... i on the other hand could not ... not ... not ... not ? ... a bubble from the deep ... one of many ... brushed by my breathlessness ... of course ! ... that was it ! ...

i lunged for my hat which had been attempting to squiggle away ... if i could collect enough of those bubbles from the deep inside my night cap ... not only would i have enough air to breath ... but i would also float safely to the surface ... bubbled up by gum ... what a plan ! ...

★ BUBBLED DOWN ★

But wait ... i thought ... hmm it would be a shame to forego such an unique opportunity as this to explore the ancient ruins of a disappeared civilization ... i hurriedly attached an anvil to my feet and bubbled down ... now that i had an unlimited supply of air from the bubbles of the deep ... i realized that i would be able to go anywhere ... if a whole civilization of ancient weasels had vanished here ... then by applying lucid intuitive rationalizing ... mathemagically speaking the chances were in my favour that i would be able to find out what happened to the one modern disappeared weasel i was trying to find out about ...

oops ... there was merVana ... tunaed into a boring fish program on the floating tube ... if she saw me i would have to hang around for hours watching some silly show on migration patterns and the ebby effects of tides ... geeztailitall ! ... then a wasted day in small talk with her catfish ... at this rate i would never make any significant discoveries ...

★ BUBBLED BACK UP ★

I decided to bubble back up again ... and cut my anvil loose ... about half way there, i think ... i thought perhaps i'm being hasty ... is not scientific discovery worth a little sacrifice of time ? ... surely i could sit through one afternoon of boring telitlikeitisntevision with merVana ... and mind numbing theorizing with the catfish ... surely ... think of the long term rewards to Weaselkind ... i reached for the spare anvil with which to bubbled back down ... but when i looked below ... i saw nothing had changed ... they were all still floundering around and totally tubed out ... i decided that maybe scientific sacrifices could be done some other time ... i tossed the extra emergency anvil and watched it fall into the depths ... it was only fishful thinking after all ... my explorations would have to wait for another day ... i bubbled back up again again ...

i broke the surface thoroughly ... nothing could stop me now ... now that i had made a decisive decision ... unless i changed my mind ... of course ... which i thought i probably wasn't going to ... but what was this ?

★ DE-ASSURED DOWN ★

This was ... another oops again ! ... i wasn't stopping ... maybe i had cap-tured too many bubbles from below into my cap ... i had been down right decisive like my self-assurance manual assured me i was to behave like ... "be assured of yourself and nothing can stop you" ... lesson 1 ... but what if i had over-done it ? what if nothing could stop me ? ... dagnabit ! ... i had seen enough of Mary's

Violet Eyes on my last trip ... i decided in a vague unconfident sort of way to de-assure down a bit ... i let out some bubbles allowing them to escape into the other atmosphere around about ...

let's see ... ethane – pink ... methane - yellow ... iso-propane - iso-green ... oxygen - green ... and nitrogen - red ... my wrist gas chromatograph never lies ... i believe ... and so letting out in just the right proportions ... say a bubble of this and a bubble of that ... i produced the precise rainbow expulsion required for a decent rate-of-descent which would result in a nice moderate landing ... what a gas i was having ... the weather was fair ... the tempest had abducted itself elsewhere ... light clouds ... unlimited visibility ... a nice window of opportunity ...

★ WINDOW OF OPPORTUNITY ★

And opportunist as i wasam ... i opened it ...swung it really ... okay ... i admit it ... i flung it ... my spirits we so high ... although i myself was coming down ...

and to raise things even more ... i saw below that my trusty tricycle trikey though cast adrift and knackered right out on its back ... had somehow managed to survive through the whirlpool and whipping winds ...

★ HOW DDO ? ★

I hit the water with great gollups of weasel gusto ... and waited for things to settle down a little ... and when they had i saw that i was looking at a whole new ball of wax game ... everything was reraragnde ? ... reardanger ? ... rangerdear ? ... rrraaeendg ? ... rearranged ... me ... my window of opportunity ... my tricycle ... and my tricycle's friend the surf board ... who dod ?... how ddo ?... how odd ... i thought ...

i could see where this was going easily enough ... i had that sudden unexplainable feeling of never having been anywhere near here before ... deja new view ... not even in a previous lifetime ... but ... what was not so oblivious was the how ddo ? how was this contraption going to fly ? the wind cap showed optimal winds and visibility was infinite ... perfect conditions to take her up ...

but come on now ... spinning tire engine props ? ... window wings ? ... those contained adequate enough inert energy to generate enough lift for a long buzz obviously ... but what if i ran out of gas ?... doesn't anybody plan ahead ?... i was all but practically out of bubbles ...

★ GUSTS AND GUTS ★

But what a doubter i turned out to be ! ... he ho ha ... i laughed at myself ... this was the new millennium of course ... no one flew with bubbles anymore ... isn't i a silly one ... nowadays everybody and weasels fly with gusts and guts ... and as i spoke ... there came a big one ...

well ... i took off ... no doubt about that at all ... but it was not really quite like i had conceived ... not at all ...

Paws 3

★ CATJACKISTAN ★

Do you feel left behind ? ... is it like the highway of life by-passed you right on by ? ... and left you pretty much down and outside counting trucks and motorhouses from the gas pumps of existence ? ... while all the jerks breeze by in their hot Weaselrattii's and Lamborweaseleenii's guzzling up precious heating fuel bubbles ? ... well son ... well daughter ... well grandweaselkids ... and cousweasels too ... remember ... there is always hope ... why not consider a career in the Unified Nests of Weaslonia Weasel Merchant Marines ... take ensign first class Weasel for example ... seen here ...

in a far off hinter-hill-land sector of hostile Catjackistan simulation ... ensign Weasel is in the field testing the new camo-bed-blanket-and-toe-warmer-battery-powered-snore-out unit ... nearly unseen under the disbelieving eyes of the enemy Catjackers ... ensign Weasel sports the proud tartan colours of his spartan home regiment ... the Weasel Highboggers ... as well as the weasel bell of determination ... will he make a sale ?? ... we can almost hear the thoughts of the enemy ... "where did they get financing for something as neat as that ?" ... "if only we overthrow our Fat Cat and embrace the UNW democratic principles of free shopping markets for all ..." "if only we loosen our boarders and all oppression is rent from our lands" ... if only ... if only ... yes if only you sign up for service in the UNW Weasel Merchant Marines ... all this and more can and might be in your future ... join while the joint's good ... the UNWWMM ...

★ TURBULENT TUMBLES ★

I was thinking more that i would have a nice smooth flight ... with time to relax ... to kick back and set the automatic-plot for a happy ending ... or at least an unbumpy landing ... now things were in turbulent tumbles ... not at all what i had anticipated forward for ...

i checked my list ... it wouldn't be easy since i had a deadline to meet ... but the mark of a true weasel is the ability to function excellently ... especially when surrounded by stress factors which would make ordinary creatures crack apart at the seamstresses ...

★ CALL ME X ★

And as usual ... i was operating on all cylinders with little to no misfiring of the capability circuits ... a phenomenal weasel talent which notably comes to the surface under the most disorderly of disruptive circumstances ... to begin with i must synopsitize my list ...

let's see now ... where could i have disappeared to ? ... i was using me as a general weasel in the baseline formula which via elasticological stretching techniques would include all weasels in the final answer ... in other words ... just call me X ...

★ A PRIORITIZED LIST ★

If i were to prioritize my hypothenooses in reverse possible order of vanishability ... then i would have ... a prioritized list of possible disappearances ... a good starting point by any measure of achievement ... they used to call me Sherlock once ... but of course that is another tail ... so ...

where have we been ? i asked of myselves ... a) ancient Egypt ... ah could i ever have been so young and weaselly ? ... i squeaked a mark with my pencil for old times sake ... b) the savannah of the Rug ... a very bad place ... i made a check after this item too ... c) the dreadful linoleum flats and the road to the Free Zer Republic ... another check here ... d) Le Cage ... awful ... torturous ... and not nice ... deserving of a check ... e) the snooze plateau and the universal tricycle express ... well a lot of unusual ground had been covered here ... but they all basically fell into the same category ... i made a definite scribble there also ... and surveyed my results ... things were coming together ... i could sense it deep within my weasel senses ... except but maybe for the occasional fish whom can never quite get things right ...

★ SWEEPY BUT EXTRAPOLATEABLE ★

Now i would have to formulate my results into a meaningful formula ... something simply extrapolateable ... i set to work ... enter X ... stage left ... that was me ... would equal ...

option (a) squared ... in honor of the Egyptian pyramid scheme ... plus or minus ... parenthesis ... option (d) cubed ... in dishonor of Le Cage which was roughly for all intense and our purposes a cube ... minus the square root of option (b) the Rug savannah ... strange plants with odd roots grew there ... then divide the lot by two times option (c) ... the linoleum flats and the Free Zer Republic ... which could be considered a double option anyway ... put all of that in brackets ... and multiply by one third the remaining option (e) ... the snooze plateau with the universal tricycle express ... this was getting interesting since there are so many variables inherent in any equation as sweepy and encompassing as this one ... but i had that old feeling again ... according to my figures there might be a remainder of one potted flower and three tropical parrot-like birds ... and/or ... one tricycle and one surf board ... or just a fish ...

★ LIMITING TO ZERO ★

And that could be disastrous ... i would in all likelihood have to find the limit as X approached zero ... which i ... being X as i was ... was hoping not to do ... lim f(x) as x approaches 0 = f(y (i)) ... the simpler the equation ... the harder it is to understand ... i knew that ... i told myself ... and i did ... fyi... but i had always hated finding the limit of a quaderratic equation ... the results were so unpredictable ... take the extra fish for instance in

the remainder ... the tropical bird digits were more or less explainable ... but another fidgit ... very difficult i knew the personal risks would be immense ... but i thought of weaselkind in general ... the benefits like my equation were all but incalculable ... just dental coverage would be beyond hyper-math ... prescriptions and general physicians were just out of the question altogether now ... i knew i had no choice ... i would have to push the limit to the outer envelope of zero ... from whence no weasel has been known to have been seen again ... i scribbled the new function on whatever and wherever it was i was ... f(x) ...

★ JUST THE F(X) PLEASE ★

Just the f(x) please ... i tried to stare it down ... but it was no good ... i was just going to have to try and understand it ... so much can be accomplished in life with a little understanding ... lucky for me too ... because i only had a little of that ... one f(x) of life most weasels learned at an early age ... the Jurassic, i think ...

but never mind that now ... if i were to ever make significant progress i would have to get down to some serious figuring ... perhaps i could take the derivative and find what was outside the mess ... or just integrate and look at the insides of it all ... i would probably reach more accuracy doing something like that ... rather than just tossing the whole dern thing out the window in one summation like i really wanted to do ... i scanned over my calculations ... while thinking i was thinking too much ... nope ... this wasn't giving the right answer at all ... it looked all wrong ...

★ RINGS A WEE BELL ★

And not only did it appear all wrong ... it also looked like work ... and too much like it too ... this rang a bit of a wee bell ... somewhere in my youthful childhood i must have done something ... i remembered ... a reed basket ... my weasel mummy's hands holding me ... gentle warm floating sensations ... oops i must have wet my diapers again ... a strange language in an ominous ancient dialect ... a trumpet and my baby bottle ... a mean and awful pharaoh threatening a 100 percent employed weasel economy ... the resultant hushed and hurried burrow borough meetings ... the catty cactus caucursings ... and the historic decision to fly ...

years ahead of their time were the ancients in those days ... not until much later ... in the year of the right great Le Cage flight did a weasel lift successfully off and into the wild blue to wander above the ground ... and ... and ... and ... i could scarcely believe the thoughts i was thinking for it seemed as if they had thoughts of their own ... i cautiously followed behind them as they snaked through the spaghetti labyrinth of my thinking ... hey ... wait a minute ... i back tracked to the wild blue yonder part ... where into which once upon a time a weasel would've ... could've ... would've ... could ... would ... did ... disappear !

★ COUP DE FINESSE ★

My thoughts returned all over me in a snap of bubbles ... my ears jumped ... i gasped an outright gasp ... great panda parched pepperoni petals ... i pealed out loud ... and squishy squirrely sqweasels too ! ... that was it ! ... off flipping course ! ... i had finally fluttered onto a fantastic final finish ! ... could my discovery be so simply true ? ... oh furry frazzled finicky fates of the fertility feast of fuzzy flowering spring blossoms ! ... what a coup de finesse ! ... what a realization ... and i had pulled it off ! ... what a weasel i thought to myself of myself ...

this was prized Nobel stuff for sure ... yes ... yes ... i could see it ... headlines in the Blank : nobel Weasel solves simmering mystery ... boils total doubts to evaporate into elusive cloud of revelations ... ethereal search ends in flabbergassed exhilaration ... all attributed to ... to ... darest i name the recipient of such acclaim ? ... should i think more uponst the matter ? ...

★ THE THREE POINT PLAN ★

Well okay ... i would ... but just a little ... all attributed to me ... weasel par excellante ... now i would have to immortalize it all down in writing before i forgot what it was ... i will refer to it here as my three (3) point plan of explanation ... in order to avoid confusion for clarifying ... 1) the quest : to find and explain the disappearance of one mr Weasel into never-to-be-seen-again land ... 2) the questions : the hows and why nuts bolt ... 3) the questionnaire : me ... i ... je ... moi ... le Weasel ... your investigator ...

i had to get serious about it all now ... this was shirt sleeve and boxer short stuff

... a very dramatic theatre de force as every weasel knows ... i tossed my cap and robe along to the nearest Cataloony griffin paw oaken coat hanger ... to begin with ... i would start by drawing heavily upon my thesis ... and also all over my baseline hypothesis that one weasel of such high calibration as you know who ... would've ... could've ... might've ... did but did not just disappear ... only by drawing on ... so could i erase all previous misconstrutions .... sort of a messy paradoxy ... i thought ... but a necessary one ...

★ USWT THE ONE POINT POSTULATION ★

It all would all have all been all too easy ... so ... let me now just snag a possible breakthrough postulation surmised from leading functions and the long ago above mentioned scientific processes ... i will call this one my one (1) point postulation ... its all apples over oranges when it drops on your head and you get it ... no need to wonder what the point is ... when there is only one ... then that's it ... you do not have to waste time understanding ... see ? ... good ... well then ... let us take 1) the universal-space-world-timeline as continuing ... umm ...

at the beginning is zero ... or all hours yesterday ... at the end is infinity ... or tomorrow and tomorrow and tomorrow and tomorrow ... which never comes due to its traveling so slowly at a creepy petty pace ... which explains why the uswt is not always a normal straight line ... gravity and sadness have much to do with this phenomenon ... but don't worry ... years of fast light and starry bright happy things also do too ... and here therefore we arrive ...   tween it all there inst lies the problem years ... often known to some as the colourful troublesome tweasel eons ...

★ THE PRESENT ★

Let us assume then that we accept the present as given ... but we'll open it now ... so here is where we find our one mr Weasel ... it was the time zero when the great plague struck over the ancient ones and for four days or nights floodlit upon them with the glaring proclamation of yon pharaoh's threat of work for all ... the elders were ripe and buzzing with the talk about if two fleas or to flee was not the questionable answer ... or whether it would be nobeler to

accept the whips and scorns of work upon their bare bodkins ... or to go to the sea of troubles with their opposing armies in the end ...

an historic decision was made ... and the wee Weasel was sent to be saved by floating in deNile until the time arrove whence he were to be gifted with some other present ...

★ TWIXT ZERO AND INFINITY ★

A simple plan you may think ... and a clever one too ... but hereinst the matter becomes slightly uncruxed ... because ... for the wee rivering Weasel deNile was wetly confusing ... and this confusion lead directly to the tangled troublesome tweasel times between never and forever ... the eons into which he disappeared in a sense from the general work force ... thereby creating a labor gap which many have mistaken for never being seen again ... but what has often been neglected in the overall analysis is this exact misconception ... for the weasel had been seen again ... in and out of deNile ... of many a sighting along the waters and shores of the universal-space-world-timeline twixt zero and infinity ... here ... let me make it simple for y'all ... i will draw a graph ...

visuals often help you to visualize things ... you see ... so we'll use the basic old xy standard two dimensional plot ... placing points of significance hither and thither ... connect 'em to make a wavy line like deNile ... and ...

★ POLAR COORDINATES ★

Let's see ... convert 'em to ... uh ... say ... polar coordinates ... thereby making a complete circle and ... and ... and ... but ... what ? ... oh my goodness golly frozen gum boobles ... what had i done ? ... yes ... well ... an oversight ... i never really liked polar coordinates because you always had to worry about pi and that led to arguments about slices and flavours ... who got what ... chocolate with coconut or lemon migraine ... and was in my opinion a headache and always a bit too much trouble to be worth the trouble you put into it ...

i realized a little too late that it was winter ... and now i had accidentally converted my hypnothesis into polar coordinates ... the circle was closed ... zero was infinity ... never was forever ... great Weasel Scott ! ... i jumped into my winter outfit ... slipped on a nice set of snow rackets ... and tossed my pencil away in discussed ... already the tip of my tail was white ... a finger was turning ... an ear was nipped ... and i had a little white diamond spot on my nose ... just like a dumb old horse ... soon all of me and my furry exterior would be changed ... and within all the swirlings of the season's snows ... by the next episode i would be all but invisible ... disappeared so to speak ... i wouldn't even have time to jump back into deNile and float away before it froze up ...

★ HIGH BRR NATION ★

Achoo-lly ... i thought with a sneeze ... this could be a blessing in disguise ... i was tired of the ancient equations ... and the numbersome graphs ... pretending to know what i was talking about and quoting the parabolas had just lead me around into circles ... this could be my big chance ... since no one would very soon be able to see me ... i could just nip off to the High Brr Nation highlands for the remainder of the winter and take in some serious snore boarding ... few realize in these days of today that once in those other days of yesterday ... i had been a very famous and well respected international snore boarder ... indeed ... and i was sure that if i showed up in persona ... i would still be esteemly remembered by the great High Brr himself ... seeing how i was a personal friend and all ...

i decided that this would be a good place to end my book ... i hit the send end button ... and lay down the plume de keyboard in the flurries of activity ... as i slowly camofrosted away into the falling snowfall of evening ... not to be seen again ...

Paws 4

★ WAWS ★

Oh dear ... is it that time again ... i do wish they would give me adequack warning ... ahem ... yes ... well ... as we all know ... the Weasel has gone and disappeared once more ... i have always thought that that type of behaviour is very underinconsidered in the whole spectrum of things in general ... but just blending away into his winter coat ? ... completely uncalled for ... and that's as far as i'm concerned ... but except for the ... well ... fare of my poor dear patients ... i wouldn't even go that far ... yes i think you know of what i speak ... weasel addicts withdrawal syndrome ... often denied ... often hidden ... and always embarrassing when it bursts upon the scene in great sobs ... waws ...

but thank our lucky enlightened weaselights ... for deep and caring advanced meditheatrical waws research continues all around the clock ... even while we talk and talk and talk ... and yak ... and jaw ... and argue ... and moan ... and go on and on and over ... even so ... progress is being made ... just in now ... and all brand new this book ... for the first time only ... available to all afflictionairies ... weasolene 2 ... the new and easy miracle drug mixture ... all previous four forms are combined ... powder ... capsules ... pills ... and ... liquid tonic ... mooshed up and squishled and ploundered and flumbered ... into this one wonderful sticky soothing easily packagable green gobby goo ... many many many simple ways

to apply it ... use the prescribed weasel flat wooden ladle (not included) ... slab it on your tongue and try to swallow ... rub it on your nose and try to lick it off ... mix it in with your tail hair for storage now and savour it later ... or just mould a nice set of booties for your feet and walk around until you knead a nibble ... use your imagination ... but remember only use the official weasel approved brand weasolene 2 ... as predescribed and certifiable as your doctor ...

★ MEDAL AWARD ★

And now ... for being such great readers and finishing Book Two of The Weasel Chronicles ... we proudly bestow uponst you a one time only presentation of this fine copy of a photograph of the Unified Nests of Weaslonia Weasel Merchant Marines Medal of Validation ... a painted bronzed image of a common UNWWMM ensign in action as suspended from the official UNW ribbon colours ... as long as you carry this de-facto authorized rendition of the medal ... you will be valid for some very stunning discounts on all available prices at numerous selected stores *

*sorry only valid if validated ...

Printed in the United States
by Baker & Taylor Publisher Services